WELCOME HOME

WELCOME HOME

MAKE YOUR HOUSE
A HEALTHY, WEALTHY, AND
HAPPY PLACE TO LIVE

· REBECCA DiLiberto ·

CHRONICLE BOOKS
SAN FRANCISCO

Library of Congress Cataloging-in-Publication Data:
DiLiberto, Rebecca.
   Welcome home : make your house a healthy, wealthy, and
happy place to live / Rebecca DiLiberto.
     p. cm.
   ISBN 978-0-8118-7733-6
   1. Feng shui. 2. Luck. 3. Feng shui in interior decoration. 4. Dwellings--Religious
aspects. I. Title. II. Title: Tips, tricks, and traditions to bring luck, prosperity, and
happiness into your life.

BF1779.F4.D55 2011
133.3'33—dc22

                                        2010016964

Manufactured in China

Designed by Working Format
Text by Rebecca DiLiberto

10 9 8 7 6 5 4 3 2 1

Chronicle Books LLC
680 Second Street
San Francisco, California 94107
www.chroniclebooks.com

TABLE OF CONTENTS

INTRODUCTION

MOST OF US DO A NUMBER OF THINGS ALMOST
instinctively when we start the process of making a new
home our own. We copy keys, we buy welcome mats.
We paint walls, hang curtains, wash windows.

But there are other, not-so-mundane, rituals that
some of us practice for more mystical reasons. Some
people won't sleep a night in a new bedroom without
placing an emerald on their bedside table to keep snakes
away—even if nary a snake has been seen in the area.
Others won't walk through the front door of their house
without first painting its threshold blue, to keep witches
from entering their sacred domestic space.

Welcome to a collection of home folklore, myth,
mystery, and fun traditions and customs from all over
the world. You don't need to believe in magic to be fasci-
nated by these superstitions. The charms and warnings
in this book will pique even a skeptic's interest—and
may even encourage her to hang a horseshoe.

This book will accompany you as you go through
the process of finding a new home, moving into it,
decorating it, starting a family, throwing parties, and

celebrating holidays and milestones. Within each chapter, rituals are classified by the sort of fortune they aim to bring, from luck to wealth to protection. Select those ideas that speak to you, and make them your own.

While most of the rituals are easy to understand and perform (barring, of course, the occasional arcane historical practice, such as mummifying cats or making owl stew), a few are drawn from customs you may not be familiar with. Here are some definitions that may be helpful before you begin reading:

Feng shui is the Chinese practice of arranging architecture and its contents to best serve the *chi*, or life force, of its inhabitants.

Vastu Shastra is a similar practice of directional alliance that stems from the Hindu tradition in India.

The real joy in this book is not necessarily found in the "magic" each superstitious practice may—or may not—bring. Pleasure will come from developing new traditions for your new home, which your family may pass from one generation to the next.

The best way to use this book is to cherry-pick your favorite rituals from the smorgasbord of superstitions and encourage your loved ones to do the same. Unlike religion, belief in charms and totems really can be a buffet.

FINDING A NEW HOME

MANY PEOPLE SPEAK OF HAVING A
sixth sense when it comes to selecting a new
place to live. Whether it is feeling pulled by some
intangible force upon seeing a "For Sale" sign,
or finding yourself on the same remote block
during your morning walk over and over again,
it's difficult to dispute that some places
exert a powerful draw on us.

It's not surprising, then, that almost every
culture has a long list of guidelines and warnings
when it comes to choosing the location of a home.
Here are some things to consider when you're
pounding the pavement trying to decide where
to put down your roots.

CHAPTER 1

CHOOSING A SITE

THE IRISH BELIEVE THAT FAIRIES
are everywhere, and that the fairies use special paths to
travel from place to place. Therefore, it's important not to build
a house on top of one of these paths. To make sure your building
site is in the clear, stake it out with four posts, then leave them
standing overnight. If, come morning, any or all of the posts have
been knocked over, you're trespassing on fairy territory, and
proceeding with construction could guarantee you
and yours a lifetime of annoyance. If the posts are
still in place, you're free to break ground.

POTENTIAL HEALTH CONCERNS
are not the only reason that you should think twice before
purchasing land near a power plant. Feng shui devotees believe
that the energy generated by the plant can actually
disrupt the flow of energy in the home.

MANY IRISH PEOPLE ALSO BELIEVE
that a family's new house should not be built directly
across the street from the old one, in order to avoid repeating
negative patterns and to ensure that the lives of everyone in the
family continue moving safely forward. Who wants to
look upon their old life when beginning anew?

WHILE MANY YOUNG FAMILIES SEEK OUT HOUSES
located in cul-de-sacs for privacy and a safe place for
their children to play, some cultures maintain that such
locations can lead to stagnation—a metaphorical dead end—
in the dwellers' lives. If you fall in love with a house on a dead-
end street, just be sure that the backyard offers lots
of open space for bodies and minds to roam.

DESIGNING A HOME

Should you be lucky enough to participate in the process of building your new abode from the ground up, consider these beliefs before signing off on those blueprints.

VASTU SHASTRA RECOMMENDS
that the entrance of a house always be placed on its northeast side. The east side of a home is ruled by the god Indra, who brings pleasure. The east is also where the sun rises, and the sunrise symbolizes new beginnings.

WHEN YOU ARE LAYING OUT THE KITCHEN,
the stove should never be visible from outside the home and should sit in the southeastern section of the kitchen. Water elements, such as the dishwasher and sink, should be in the northeastern part.

WHEN PLANNING THE LOCATION OF THE BEDROOMS
in your new home, consider that, in Filipino culture,
the master bedroom ideally has a window
facing east. Filipinos believe that this
allows God's grace to come in.

SOME FENG SHUI MASTERS MAINTAIN
that a master bedroom with an adjoining bathroom can cause
digestion problems in the occupants. Should this be the
case for you, at least there's a bathroom close by!

BATHROOMS SHOULD FACE EAST,
because the morning light is believed to promote health,
says the Vastu Shastra doctrine.

ACCORDING TO INDONESIAN TRADITION
the construction of an indoor pool can lead to illness.

FENG SHUI PRACTICE ESPOUSES

a number of specifications regarding a new home, such as:

No home should face north.

Bedrooms should not be placed over a garage.

Bathrooms should not be situated over dining rooms.

Two doors should not face one another.

The color red brings nothing but luck, prosperity,
and happiness everywhere you put it.

Every staircase should have an even number of steps.

BUT VASTU SHASTRA, A HINDU BELIEF SYSTEM

similar to feng shui, maintains that staircases should
always have an odd number of steps, so that one can both start
and finish on the right foot. Luckily, there's a tradition to
validate your staircase, however many steps it has!

BUYING A HOME

ACCORDING TO FENG SHUI,
it's never a good idea to choose a home site below
street level, as the placement of the entrance can
make it difficult for chi to enter the house.

AVOID MOVING TO A LOWER FLOOR
in an apartment building, as some believe this downward
mobility could portend a decrease in earnings.

LOOK FOR A HOME WITH A PATH
that winds gently from the street to the entrance
instead of in a harsh straight line. A more meandering path
gives the house's occupant more time to linger and
discover all that life has to offer.

A STRONG FOUNDATION

*If you are fortunate enough to build your home
from your own specifications, here are some tips
to heed when breaking ground.*

Some eastern cultures believe it is best to begin
construction when the moon is full, but devotees of
astrology say the time to start is during the new moon,
since it symbolizes rebirth and new beginnings.

In Turkey, during the pouring of the
foundation, a sheep is sometimes sacrificed as a
gesture of thanks to the Almighty. If you are able to
attend the foundation pouring but have no sheep to
sacrifice, toss a few coins in with the concrete, and your
life in the home will be prosperous as long as
the coins remain under the house.

In Thailand, it is traditional to wrap gold or money in the leaves of a water lily, then place it at the base of the foundation before the concrete is poured. This ensures that the occupants of the house will be prosperous.

In Ireland, the custom is to bury in the foundation coin that was minted in the same year that the home is built, to encourage prosperity. The Irish have also been known to throw in a few religious totems, such as vials of holy water, religious pictures, or saints' medals.

MOST FILIPINOS WILL NOT BUY

even the most spectacular home if it has a staircase
that leads out the front door, believing that all the wealth
will flow directly out of the house. They will also not buy
a home located on a T-shaped intersection, one whose metal
address numbers are hung on a downward slope, or one
sold in the aftermath of a divorce. These things
could lead to bad luck for the occupants.

THINK TWICE ABOUT BUYING A HOME

with visible cracks through the doorstep, since this can be a
sign of instability (both figuratively and literally!).

DON'T OPT FOR A HOUSE

that has a bathroom at its center, since in feng shui
the center of a house represents its health and, by extension, the
health of the family. All that flushing isn't exactly . . . serene.

SELLING A HOME

Chances are, if you're in the process of selecting a new home, you're likely looking to rid yourself of an old one. Here are some ways to be sure you have the proceeds in hand from your old house in time to shell out a down payment on the new one.

MAKE SURE THE STOVE BURNERS ARE CLEAN.
Besides the obvious sanitary turn-off, food remnants will remind potential buyers of who used to live in the home. Subconsciously they may find it difficult to imagine their own family in a kitchen that seems to belong to someone else.

PUT VIBRANT, THRIVING PLANTS
in the back left corner of as many rooms as possible. This will energize the space and create a feeling of vitality.

If you have a cat, bring it to visit the property you're considering. Many believe that your cat knows your tastes better than you do—and that he or she may be able to sense the presence of unsavory spirits.

ELIMINATE ALL CLUTTER,

and open up tight furniture arrangements. This will maximize the channels through which energy can flow unfettered through the home.

BURY A SMALL STATUE OF ST. JOSEPH

facing the street, near your "For Sale" sign. Situate him so he's upside-down and facing the front of your home. No one seems to be sure why the statue must be St. Joseph, but he is the patron saint of carpenters, so perhaps his presence will ensure that your old house doesn't fall apart before it sells!

WRITE THE WORD "SOLD" ACROSS A PHOTOGRAPH

or copy of your home's real estate listing, and look at it frequently. This trick may help manifest a quick sale by convincing you—even if just for a second—that the sale has already taken place. Many modern self-help traditions are built on this idea of self-suggestion—that we are capable of creating our own realities.

MOVING INTO A NEW HOME

NO MATTER WHAT YOUR BELIEF SYSTEM, it's hard to deny that a house is changed by its owners—this is how a mere building becomes a true home. And when we leave a house, we undoubtedly leave behind a bit of our lives there. Consequently, it is important to cleanse and purify a previously occupied home before moving into it. In addition to any spiritual benefits, starting with a clean slate can positively impact your family's psychological well-being. This section will tell you how to begin the process of symbolically making a new home your own.

DON'T BOTHER SWEEPING OUT YOUR OLD HOUSE
after you've removed your belongings. What is left
there should remain—it's not meant to be stirred up
and carried into your new life. (Plus, by sweeping, you'll
be denying the house's new occupants the pleasure
of symbolically ushering out your detritus and
creating a clean slate for themselves.)

THE DAY OF THE WEEK ON WHICH YOU MOVE
is important, too. According to Tamil culture,
moving on a Thursday will bode well for your life in your
new home. Fridays and Saturdays are not as lucky.

IN INDIA, A BRIDE USUALLY WALKS
into her new home on her own two feet, instead of
being carried. But in order to start off on the metaphorical
right foot, so to speak, she must always enter
with her (literal) right foot first.

If you can, choose a move-in day when the moon is waxing. If the moon is experiencing a stage of growth rather than shrinkage, your new life will also be on the upswing.

A GROOM SHOULD CARRY HIS BRIDE
over the threshold of their new home so that she does
not trip or fall—talk about an inauspicious start to a new life!
But consider this as well: by symbolically keeping a bride
off the ground, her new husband can protect her from
any evil beings gathering at the door. (Not to
mention "sweeping her off her feet"; a nice
precedent to set for a happy life.)

GERMANS BELIEVE THAT IF A BRIDE
brings a piece of her mother's dishcloth with her
to the house where she will live with her husband,
she will never be homesick.

ENTER YOUR HOME FOR THE FIRST TIME
through the front door, not the back one.
This symbolizes forward movement.

ITALIANS SWEEP OUT A NEW HOME

with a new broom before moving in their belongings,
in order to cleanse the space of negative energy. They
believe that dirt can trap whatever the previous occupants
wanted to leave behind, so it's best to sweep it all away. Then
they sprinkle salt—or a few drops of a solution of ¼ cup of
sea salt dissolved in 1 cup of water—into the corners of
each room. If you wish to purify the outdoor areas of
your new home, use cornmeal rather than salt,
as salt can find its way to the earth around
your home and render it inarable.

BURY FOUR CRYSTALS OF PURE QUARTZ

around the perimeter of your home at the four compass
points—north, south, east, and west.

To rid a home of the ghosts of former residents,
the Scottish believe the new owners should walk
through each room clashing cymbals, as the loud,
sudden noise will scare spirits out. (Try not to
worry about what your neighbors will think,
though you may want to reassure them
that you're not starting a family
marching band.)

WALK THROUGH YOUR HOME

wielding a burning sage stick—often called a "smudge stick"
in the Native American tradition. The smoke generated by
burning sage is said to chase out any negative energy remaining
from the previous inhabitants. Don't forget the closets!
(And don't forget to keep an extinguisher nearby, just in case.)

IF THE HOME'S PREVIOUS OWNERS

are particularly altruistic (or superstitious), they will leave
basic kitchen staples for you, to symbolize abundance. If the
cupboards are bare in your new home, bring some symbolic
foodstuffs—flour, rice, sugar, or whatever holds meaning
for you and your family—before you move in. This will
ensure that your family always has enough to eat.

ON MOVE-IN DAY, SCATTER HANDFULS OF COINS—

real or imaginary—around the living room. This expansive
gesture will set the stage for prosperity
that is more than just symbolic.

PLANT AN OAK TREE IN THE YARD
and place red flowering plants along the walkway leading
up to the front door. The oak tree symbolizes
stability; the plants, wealth.

AS TEMPTING AS IT MAY BE TO HAMMER NAILS
into the wall well into the wee hours when you first
move into a house, resist the urge to hang pictures
after dark. Some cultures warn that doing so
angers the tree gods, and this could lead
to problems in your garden.

WHEN YOU LEAVE YOUR NEW HOME
for the first time, be sure to exit through the same door
through which you entered. Some think that if you fail
to do so, you will never settle comfortably.

BEDROOMS

IT IS IMPERATIVE FOR A BEDROOM DOOR
to open and close freely and not be restricted in any
way. According to Vastu Shastra, the bedroom doorway
represents all the possibility and opportunity ahead of
a person, and so it must be as open as possible to
help good things come to fruition. Accordingly, try
to avoid placing a clothing hook on the back
of a bedroom door. This usually prevents
the door from opening fully.

NEWLYWEDS SHOULD ENSURE
that their bedrooms have at least one east-
facing window. Since the sun rises in the east,
the couple will be reminded daily of the new
beginnings that await them.

TRIM LARGE TREES THAT ENCROACH
upon windows. Not only do they block light, but they
can make the room's occupant feel oppressed.

SOME FENG SHUI PRACTITIONERS RECOMMEND
that you sleep with your head pointing east, so that the
morning light hits it before any other part of your body,
but Vastu Shastra suggests you orient your head toward the
south in order to harness positive energy coming from the north.
The direction that everyone seems to agree your sleeping head
should not face is west. There's no need for a compass—
just keep your feet toward the sunset.

THE HEADBOARD OF YOUR BED
should not share a wall with a bathroom, since your bed
is meant to be a space of renewal, and the bathroom
is a place to wash away impurities.

TO BANISH SERPENTS, SCATTER SOLOMON'S SEAL,
a plant in the lily family that can be found in the
American Midwest, over the floor. Thankfully, most of us
don't battle snake infestations on a regular basis.
Solomon's seal can banish whatever a
serpent represents to you or your family—
fears, bad dreams, intruders, or sneaky tricksters.

TRY NOT TO POSITION YOUR BED
directly underneath a slanted portion of your ceiling,
as this could stifle energy and compromise your health.
If you must, hang some wind chimes from a rafter or the ceiling
to generate positive energy in this congested space.

NEVER POSITION A TELEVISION OR A MIRROR
directly across from your bed. Those who believe the soul is
distinct from the body hold that the soul might see its image in
the reflective surface when the body is asleep, and
be startled and emotionally scarred for life.

THOSE OF US WHO GREW UP IN CITIES
don't always realize that lightning can enter your home
through a windowpane. To keep this from happening, hang
mistletoe in the window—and not just at Christmastime. To
prevent yourself from getting shocked by any lightning
entering your home through pipes or wires, be sure
not to touch anything metal during a storm.

IF A BEDROOM IS A PLACE FOR WORK
or study, never position a desk so that the person sits
with his or her back facing the door. The person at the
desk should face east; according to Vastu Shastra,
this improves concentration.

Too many sharp angles in a bedroom can lead
to feelings of stress and constriction. Consider
angling your bed slightly so it's not in perfect
alignment with all the room's right angles,
or place plants in each corner of the
room to soften the energy.

– BABIES' AND CHILDREN'S ROOMS –

NEVER PLACE A BABY'S CRIB
against a wall shared by a bathroom or storage room,
as this could negatively affect the baby's health.

AVOID USING THE AREA UNDER A CRIB
or bed for storage. Energy must be able to circulate
freely through this space.

IF YOUR BABY IS HAVING TROUBLE SLEEPING
through the night, feng shui doctrine suggests orienting
the crib so the baby's head faces north.

IF YOU WANT YOUR CHILDREN TO SLEEP SOUNDLY
and maximize their powers of concentration, their
bedrooms should not be located in the
southwest corner of the house.

PLACE ALL THE FURNITURE IN A CHILD'S ROOM
at least a few inches from the wall. Putting it flush
against the wall can congest the flow of positive energy.

CHILDREN, LIKE FLOWERS,
need as much natural light and fresh air as possible
in order to grow. Keep window coverings open during
the day, and decorate windowsills and the dark
corners of their rooms with leafy green plants.

SLEEPING SOUNDLY

It is said that whatever transpires in your dreams
during the first night you sleep in your new home
will come to pass while you live there. These
tips will ensure your dreams are good ones.

Hanging a Native American dream catcher in
the bedroom of someone who suffers
from nightmares will trap the bad dreams,
robbing them of their power to scare.

Position your bed so that moonlight does
not shine upon your face. Some believe this
can cause your facial features—or your
sanity—to become distorted.

Children are likely as terrified of nightmares
as witches are of horses, as mentioned on page 81.
Luckily, hanging a horseshoe above the bed will
chase bad dreams into the ether.

To prevent nightmares, place your shoes
under the edge of your bed with
the toes pointing away from you.

According to British tradition, sleeping
with the open side of your pillowcase facing
out will banish terrifying dreams.

The Irish believe that a dream dreamt
while lying on your right side will come true.

LIVING ROOM

PLACE SOFAS AGAINST THE SOUTH
or west walls, so they do not block the energy coming
from the east (which represents newness and possibility).
If a sofa must be aligned with the east wall, be sure to
leave a few inches of clear space around it in
every direction to encourage flow.

WHEN PEOPLE VISIT, SENIOR FAMILY MEMBERS
should always be situated facing north or east, and
guests facing west or south. Facing north or east
puts the elders in a position of honor, which
will maximize their exposure
to positive energy.

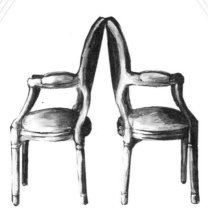

*Placing two chairs with their backs against
each other is lucky. Presumably, this position
is symbolic: when family members press
up against one another, they can
support each other with
very little effort.*

GHOST BUSTERS

Children aren't the only ones who are terrified of ghostly intruders—their parents are, too. Here are some ways to banish these ethereal invaders, whether or not you're willing to admit you're afraid of them.

When candlelight burns blue, you may be in the presence of visitors from another realm.

Should you encounter an unwanted ghost in your bedroom, walk around it nine times to make it disappear. Or, crow like a rooster so the night dweller is fooled into thinking the sun is about to come up.

Be careful never to slam your bedroom door—
whether you're bolting from a room in fear or simply
making a point in an argument—as you could hurt a
ghost, who would then have reason to haunt you.

Metal objects can be wielded as a charm against
ghosts—some people believe that anything made
of steel will keep them away, while Bengalis
believe that iron objects work best.

Some say that ghosts will vacate the premises
if you take the door to the room they favor off
its hinges, move the hinges to the other side
of the jamb (so the door opens in the opposite
direction), and then reattach the door.

SOME TRADITIONS MAINTAIN THAT EXPOSED BEAMS
can create feelings of stress in living rooms,
as they can impede the smooth flow of energy
along the ceiling. Try to avoid situating furniture directly
beneath beams, and divert any unproductive
energy by aiming lights up at them.

IF YOU WORRY THAT AN UNFAMILIAR GUEST
might bring mischief or negativity into your home,
burn incense to keep any bad energy away.

BECAUSE OF THEIR TRANSPARENT NATURE,
windows are believed to be an easy way for negativity to enter
a home. To mystify bad entities, tie back your curtains
with tassels or fringes. (You can also hang them on
doorknobs or furniture for a similar effect.)

JUST AS WEARING A BLUE BEADED NECKLACE
is a charm against ill will, so is a blue beaded
pillow tossed on a sofa.

ON PALM SUNDAY, GATHER SOME BRANCHES
from a hazel tree and put them in a vase of water.
Set them on a table near a window to prevent lightning
from coming in for the rest of the year. Or put an acorn
in your living room window to banish lightning.

IF YOU WISH TO KEEP A CERTAIN EVIL SPIRIT
from entering your home, hang its image on a door
or window, facing out. Employ this tactic with an
image of the devil, your home's previous
occupant, or even a lit cigarette.

WHEN YOU FEEL AFRAID,
create a circular space in your home as a refuge—
evil spirits will not be able to penetrate it. Putting together
this "safe place" can be easy and fun—start with a circular area
rug and arrange a chain of comfy floor pillows around
its perimeter. Or simply place furniture around a
central point for a more subtle sanctuary.

IF YOU CAN FIND THE RARE PIECE OF BAMBOO
whose center is not hollow, display it prominently
in your living room—it will attract only good
things and repel bad ones.

IN SPAIN, ANTLERS ARE BELIEVED TO PROTECT
against the evil eye. Hang a pair in your living room to
keep it safe from beings that might wish
to harm you or your family.

DINING ROOM

THE HEAD OF THE HOUSEHOLD

should face east when seated at the dining table.

The energy that flows from the east represents rebirth, and

the person facing this energy sits in a place of honor.

WHEN DINING WITH EXTENDED FAMILY,

serve the oldest people at the table first—

Indonesians believe this will benefit their

health, and yours as well.

PLACE A WARM LAMP

in the southeast corner of the dining

room to encourage conviviality among those guests

who don't know one another, and to guard

against explosive arguments.

IN ORDER TO PREVENT ARGUMENTS
over dinner, make sure that the dining room table
always has an even number of chairs. This practice
seems to be dictated as much by common sense as by
superstition—with an even number of guests, there's
no "odd man out." But it also relates back to the
Last Supper, when thirteen guests—an
odd number—represented the
beginning of the end.

CHOOSE A SOOTHING WATER ELEMENT
to grace the dining room, such as a fountain
or an aquarium. Try to place it on the north side
of the room, centered against the wall. If you prefer
not to take this suggestion literally, a piece of artwork
depicting water works well, too. The calming aura
of water is believed to aid digestion and
contribute to friendly conversation.

KITCHEN

Virtually every culture regards the kitchen as the heart of the home. This is likely because, since the dawn of modern civilization, the kitchen has been the room that contains the stove—the source of fire that warms the family and keeps it fed. (Have you ever noticed that, no matter how big a house is, everybody always congregates in the kitchen during a party?) Accordingly, the vibe in one's kitchen must be just right, or the energy of the whole house could suffer.

THE HOUSE'S MAIN COOK SHOULD try to face east when cooking. As with eating and sleeping, facing east helps maximize the positive energy a person receives.

ANIMAL MAGNETISM

Try these animal talismans to bring luck:

Hang a picture of a "trunk-up" white elephant facing toward your front door. This became a tradition during the Great Depression and, while no one is sure why, speculation is that it is because white elephants in Thailand received a lot of media attention at the time for their exclusiveness and expensive upkeep. Accordingly, people hang a photograph of a white elephant hoping to attract a similar vibe of leisure and prosperity to their home.

A warning: while peacock feathers are
a popular decorating motif, some insist that
they are unlucky and should not be brought inside
the home, as their pattern resembles an
infinite number of evil eyes.

Keep a rabbit's foot–real or synthetic–
in your makeup case for luck, as British actors do.
It's not clear whether this tradition originated with
African animism or with the Christian Easter holiday
(in which the "bunny rabbit" represents rebirth),
but it lives on in theaters (and pockets)
all over the world.

VASTU SHASTRA ASSERTS

that a balance must be maintained between
fire and water energies in the kitchen—which makes
sense literally as well as figuratively. Accordingly, if you have
only one stove and one sink, you're golden. But if you collect
countertop cookers, toaster ovens, or plug-in grills, you're
going to want to add a few more water elements to
balance things out. Try lining your kitchen window
with some thirsty plants, or investing in an
eco-friendly soda-making machine.

TRY TO AVOID STORING ANYTHING

above the stove—this area should be clear in order
to easily let out smoke and exhaust. This is not only for
obvious safety reasons, but also because smoke contains the
elements of food that are not meant to be eaten, and being
exposed to them is unhealthy not only for one's lungs
but also for one's overall energy balance.

ACCORDING TO FENG SHUI PRACTICE,
hanging a mirror over the stove encourages prosperity.

OR, IF YOU PREFER, HANG A BAG OF SALT
behind the stove in a brand-new house to bring good luck.
No one seems to know why this Southern tradition
works, but many claim it does.

GREEKS AND ITALIANS HANG BRAIDS OF GARLIC
in their kitchens not only to use in their cooking
but also to ward off bad energy.

GROW DILL
in a kitchen herb garden to repel negativity.

COLOR THEORY

*Certain colors can be a boon to certain rooms. These tips
will help you determine the luckiest color scheme.*

Many regard blue as a magical color.
There's an old saying, "Touch blue, and your
wish will come true." So why not create a special
wishing spot for your family in one of the
shared rooms of your home?

Painting the dining room pink or orange,
according to Vastu Shastra, will stimulate the
family's appetite. Perhaps, like many of us, you have
the opposite objective—to encourage family members
to eat a little bit less. If that's the case, opt for a blue
dining room, according to feng shui practice.

Indian tradition recommends a cool
and calming color scheme for the living room,
such as shades of blue, green, and white. Since the
living room is a place where people of various ages
and viewpoints gather, a tranquil scheme
discourages discord.

According to feng shui, an excellent choice
for a kitchen color combination is white
with green accents. This boosts health
and promotes the freshness of food.

Painting your bathroom bright red will
lead to wealth, according to feng shui tradition.
Other good colors are blue, gray, and white.

Place an onion on your kitchen windowsill
to absorb hurtful energy. Place a bulb
of garlic there to attract health.

SPRINKLE A PINCH OF WELL-SIFTED WHITE FLOUR
at the back of a kitchen cabinet to encourage abundance.

KEEP A FULL GLASS OF WATER
on top of your refrigerator to drown any evil spirits
who may be lurking in the kitchen.

SOME FRENCH PEOPLE KEEP AN EGG
that was laid on Good Friday in their icebox all year,
believing it possesses a strong ability to
prevent and extinguish fire.

IN CANADA, IT IS BELIEVED
that washing a plate that was used to bring you food
is bad luck for the giver. Instead, return it dirty.
This means it will always be overflowing.

ONE ALLEGHENY BELIEF IS
that an apron worn upside down is bulletproof.
Since, thankfully, not many of us worry about fending off
gunfire while we're making dinner, some people may choose
to take this "armor" idea metaphorically. Perhaps you anticipate
having a disagreement with a spouse or child or are planning to
make a particularly treacherous chicken dish. Whatever
your kitchen opponent is, your upside-down apron
may render you "bulletproof."

A YIDDISH TRADITION IS TO GIVE SALT,
sugar, and flour to new homeowners to balance the
bitterness, sweetness, and substance of their new lives.
(Drop hints to your friends and family.)

STASHING A JAR OF ALFALFA
in a kitchen cabinet will ensure that the
cabinet never goes bare.

BATHROOM

NEVER LEAVE A TOILET LID UP
when you are not using it. Feng shui practitioners believe
that an open toilet can literally suck your home's energy
down the drain, flushing it away forever.

VASTU SHASTRA WARNS AGAINST
the use of dark colors in the bathroom, which should
always appear bright and clean. If you can't avoid a
dark-colored sink, tub, or tilework, make sure your
walls are bright and freshly painted, and
fill the room with plants.

FENG SHUI DICTATES THAT THE BATHROOM
always be spotless and brightly lit. If you fail to keep it that
way, you risk the health of everyone who uses it.

GARDEN

TRADITIONAL GREEK LORE SAYS
that a cutting will not prosper into a full-grown plant
unless it is taken from someone else's property.

TO CULTIVATE LARGE CUCUMBERS,
enlist the help of a man while planting.

ALTHOUGH ITALIANS BELIEVE
that a yucca plant can bring happiness, it should
be kept outside, never brought into the home
(which could produce the opposite effect).

NEVER SAY "THANK YOU"
when someone gives you seeds, or they will fail to grow.

VEGETABLES THAT GROW ABOVE GROUND
should be planted when the moon is waxing for best
results; those that grow underground should
be planted when it's waning.

NEVER FLICK DIRT TOWARD THE HOUSE
while you're digging, as doing so brings bad luck.

SOW NORTH TO SOUTH
rather than east to west—this is believed to
produce more robust seed growth.

IN SOME PARTS OF THE CARIBBEAN,
it is thought to be a bad idea to pick fruit after dark,
lest you rob the tree of its sleep. If you own fruit
trees, harvest them in the daytime.

FINISHING TOUCHES

Once you've completed your basic layout and decor, these tips will help bring a little more luck and protection.

Always nestle a pillow in a rocking chair;
it's unlucky for a rocking chair to be empty. In old
American folklore, movement in a vacant rocking chair
was evidence of death, or that a spirit was about.

A fashionable trend in home decor is to
paint stripes or checkerboard patterns on hardwood
or concrete floors. Afghan tradition warns against
doing this, however, because it can lead to debt.
(No wonder they have such gorgeous rugs.)

If you have a fireplace, build a fire.
Each time you poke the fire, it will bring more luck.

If you keep candles in your home, more often
than not they should be lit. For many cultures, an
extinguished candle is a sign of premature
death, while a burning flame represents life.

PROTECTING AND MAINTAINING YOUR HOME

MOST OF US WOULDN'T CONSIDER
spending even one night in a house
without locks on the doors, but did you
know that some people insist on drawing a
circle around the perimeter of their home with
sea salt before they can relax? They believe
this creates a realm of positive energy
that evil spirits cannot penetrate.
Read on for more ways to keep
your family protected.

OUTSIDE

SUSPEND AN EMPTY HORNET'S NEST
from a high exterior point on your house. I challenge
you to find an intruder—beast or human—who is not a little bit
terrified of a swarm of hornets. Remember, you are
the only one who knows that this particular
hornet's nest is empty.

TRAIN IVY TO GROW
on the exterior walls of your house. This lush
green plant will blanket your home in ribbons of
positive energy, keeping negativity out.

HANG WHITE AND YELLOW PIECES
of cloth from a tree in your front yard to make your
property inhospitable for evil spirits.

Encourage swallows to nest in the eaves of your
new home. Each time they return in spring, you'll
be newly protected from bad weather—and bad
energy. To do this, build a small nesting box—you
can find instructions and materials at your local
hardware store—and place it 10 to 15 feet off
the ground. Be patient as you wait for the
swallows; you may have to try a few
different locations before they
make the box their home.

PUT A MARBLE STATUE SOMEWHERE
near your home to assert the strength of your own
little society. One reason that you see so many marble
statues in Italy is that their hardiness appealed to
Renaissance civilizations, representing the
staying power of their cities.

RENAISSANCE-ERA ITALIANS BELIEVED
that burying a bronze or stone equestrian statue helped
defend a city from war and plunder. Why not protect your
own family the same way? This is an especially brilliant
strategy if you should receive a housewarming gift
that you'd rather "display" underground,
rather than out in the open.

IF YOU DRAW A CHALK LINE
across your driveway, the devil won't be
able to penetrate your home.

PLANT HOUSELEEK ON YOUR ROOF —
this succulent, flowering plant will keep your house
from catching on fire. This special plant also serves
as a powerful reminder of the resiliency of
nature; its Latin name, *Sempervivum,*
means "live forever."

JAPANESE SHINTO SHRINES ARE PROTECTED
by a pair of *Shishis,* mythical creatures that are a
combination of a lion and a dog. Place statues
of your favorite ferocious animals on each
side of your front door to protect your own family.

TO KEEP THE ENERGY IN YOUR HOME PURE,
Shinto tradition suggests sprinkling water around your front
gate in the morning and evening to symbolize cleanliness.
If you don't have a front gate, sprinkle water
where your property begins.

ENTRANCE

FENG SHUI TRADITION DICTATES
hanging a wind chime near your home's entrance in
order to attract chi and repel negativity. Hang the
chime on the side of the door that opens—
not the hinged side—to usher energy in.

RUB SOME PURE OLIVE OIL
on the doorjambs while saying a blessing that
is meaningful to you. This practice stems from
the ancient Christian tradition of anointing, which
signifies the presence of God and the
purification of evil forces.

MAKE A SACHET OF RED ONIONS,
dried chili peppers, and turmeric and suspend it above
your front door to ward off black magic.

SOME JAPANESE HOMES
and businesses hang braided ropes called
shimenawa on their front doors to signify purity and
ward off evil. Although traditional shimenawa are made of
straw ropes braided together, you can use any kind of rope. Once
you've made a large braid, hang it like a banner across the top
of your doorway. Then you can hang any protective
charms that are meaningful to you from
the piece of draped rope.

THE HAWAIIANS CALL THE CORDYLINE,
or Ti plant, "Good Luck Plant." Accordingly, they
plant it to the right of the entrance to their homes.
To the left they plant "Heavenly Bamboo," a.k.a. *Nandina
Domestica*. This flowering plant, which is related to barberry,
is believed in most Asian traditions to bring
prosperity and safety to a new home.

TO KEEP AWAY THE EVIL EYE,
place a cactus near the front entrance of your home.
The Greeks believe its sharp thorns threaten anyone who
desires to harm the home's inhabitants.

SOME GREEK FAMILIES HANG AN IMAGE
of an eye over the front door to banish any feelings
of envy in family members or guests.

THE ROMANS BELIEVED
that evil would stay out if forced to pass
over an open pair of scissors. So bury an open pair
under your doorstep. If the safety concerns that
accompany this ritual give you pause, you can always
bury a picture of an open pair of scissors—or
even design your own doormat, with open
scissors printed on the underside.

Plant some clover near the front door.
Sure, the four-leafed kind is lucky, but the
garden variety also brings protection.

Hang a bell over the entrance to your home. The clear clang it produces will send evil beings running.

HIGH AND HIDDEN PLACES

HANG AN EVERGREEN BRANCH

from the rafters to make anything unlucky feel unwelcome.

SUSPEND A SNAKESKIN

from the rafters to keep your home from catching on fire.

PLACE A CHILD'S SHOE IN THE CHIMNEY

or attic of your house to keep bad spirits out. This tradition
originated in nineteenth-century Australia, but you can do it too.

IN OLD ENGLAND, PEOPLE WERE KNOWN

to hide a mummified cat under the floorboards. They believed
that this prevented evil forces from entering their homes. A
ferocious, living pet would seem to be just as effective, however.

WITCH CRAFTY

Anyone who's seen **The Wizard of Oz** *knows that, as with any subset of humankind, there are both good and bad witches. Here are a number of ways to keep the vicious ones from paying your new home a visit (don't worry, they won't keep Glinda away):*

Witches cannot pass over cold metal.
So hide a knife under your doormat, or use
the scissors tip mentioned on page 76.

Paint your threshold blue.

Plant a bay tree in your front yard.

Keep a broom outside your front door.
Legend says that a witch will have to count
each bristle before entering your house and, by
the time she's finished, the Witching Hour
will have long since passed.

Hang a sachet of dried fennel above the
threshold, or cultivate a bunch of
rosemary near your new abode.
Bad witches are averse to these smells.

A horseshoe suspended points-up above
the front door will scare bad witches away,
as they are terrified of horses. In fact, many
believe that a bad witch who attempts to
walk under a horseshoe will melt.

PREPARING FOR WEATHER

Prepare for rain if . . .

A cow lifts its tail

Cattle collect close together on low ground

Ants go wild

Chimney smoke travels straight up

A cat sneezes

Dogs scratch wildly

A donkey brays or twitches its ears

Ducks quack with more passion than usual

A ring appears around the moon

A rainbow materializes in the west

Batten down the hatches for a storm if . . .

A cat relaxes with its back to the fire

A cock crows in the evening

The sun will soon shine when . . .

Cattle spread out on high ground

Bats frolic in the daytime

Sheep recline comfortably

A rainbow appears in the east

WHEN FROGS CROAK WILDLY

after a rain, the rain will not return for a while.

CHECK YOUR MILK AFTER A THUNDERSTORM —

the booms and crackles might cause it to sour.

SOME BELIEVE THAT KNITTING on the doorstep during the wintertime lengthens the bitterest season. In Iceland, your neighbors will likely become peeved if they catch you doing so.

———⌇———

YOU PROBABLY KNOW IT'S BAD LUCK to open an umbrella indoors, but in the Philippines this belief is held for a very specific reason: the umbrella is believed to cause centipedes to rain from the ceiling!

———⌇———

COUNT HOW MANY FOGS APPEAR IN AUGUST— there will be the same number of snowstorms in winter. If you live in a climate where it doesn't snow, there's no need to count fogs (unless, of course, you enjoy it).

CLEANING AND MAINTENANCE

*You can find satisfaction not only in the results
of your housekeeping but in the practice of it as well.
Two accomplished British authors spoke of its benefits:
"The best time for planning a book is while
you're doing the dishes," said Agatha Christie.
And D. H. Lawrence reminisced, "I got the blues
thinking of the future, so I left off and made some
marmalade. It's amazing how it cheers one up
to shred oranges and scrub the floor."*

*The following suggestions may do more
than inspire a mystery story or cure a bad mood.
Read on to find out how to conjure luck
with a dirty dishtowel.*

THE FIRST TIME YOU USE A NEW BROOM,
sweep some dust from outside the front
door into the house to usher in luck.

NEVER SWEEP DUST AND DEBRIS
you've collected with a broom directly out the door, or you'll
be sweeping out your luck as well. Instead, sweep
it into a dustpan and carry it outside.

A SINGLE WOMAN WHO SWEEPS
away a cobweb hanging directly over her head will
soon have a new love. In fact, she should be sure to
sweep away all the cobwebs in her house,
or she might never marry.

SWEEP IN THE MORNING,
not at night.

Speaking of brooms, you should neither borrow nor lend one. Brooms carry with them all the metaphorical dust of their owners, and this detritus should not be passed around.

IF YOU ACCIDENTALLY BREAK A DISH
or cup when washing up, break another one on
purpose, or be extra careful with the rest, as
another will be prone to breaking.

BURY A DIRTY DISHTOWEL
in your backyard during the full moon.
Don't worry, you're not meant to unearth this
soiled rag at any point. It will bring luck to your
property for as long as it is buried there.

TO BANISH BEDBUGS OR FLEAS,
capture some on a piece of paper or index
card, then trap and seal the critters in a plastic bag.
Bring the pests to a nearby park or other public space
where they're unlikely to cause harm, and a mass
migration of all their compatriots
will soon follow.

CLEANING OUT YOUR CLOSETS
once a year is an important ritual. But
before donating or throwing away old clothing,
wash it, or you could be passing on your
unfinished business and/or bad luck
to unsuspecting new owners.

NEVER LET TRASH STAY
in wastebaskets too long—this can interrupt
the flow of energy throughout the home and keep
new things—both literal and figurative—
from coming in.

TIGHTEN BANISTERS AND HANDRAILS
whenever they become even a little bit loose.
Hanging on to something that is insecurely
anchored can produce feelings of fear,
which in turn can attract misfortune.

Bringing Love and Family into Your Home

WHETHER YOU'VE FOUND YOUR
soul mate or are still searching, your
home environment greatly contributes
to the success of your relationship—or the
lack thereof. Not to mention that clues to
your romantic destiny can be found in
the most mundane corners of your life.
Read on to find or strengthen
your perfect match.

FINDING LOVE

ALWAYS FINISH WHAT YOU START—
especially if what you've started is a quilt or bedspread.
Some believe that those who begin these projects but
fail to complete them will never marry, either.

AN UNMARRIED WOMAN MAY PREDICT
the character of her future spouse by the kinds of birds
that visit her home on Valentine's Day. A sparrow
signals a blissful marriage to a penniless person.
A goldfinch predicts a union with a wealthy bachelor.
And a robin? The lady must ready herself for a life on
the open seas, for she will marry a sailor.

SWEEPING THE FLOORS AT NIGHT
may bring a visit from a man.

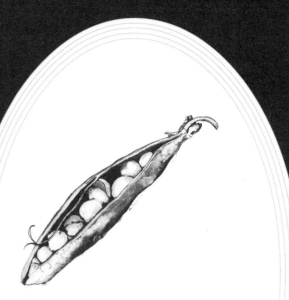

If, when shelling peas, you open a pod
with nine peas in it, hang it from the top
of your front doorjamb so that visitors must
pass underneath it. The next person
to walk through will be the
one you marry.

ACCORDING TO FILIPINO BELIEF,
a single person who takes the last piece of food
from a platter may be single forever.

WHEN BAKING A PIE, PEEL AN APPLE
in one long motion, then toss the peel over your
left shoulder. The letter it forms upon landing
will be the initial of your true love.

IF, ON A FIRST OR SECOND DATE,
you invite a new prospect over for tea, and bubbles
appear around the perimeter of a teacup,
you two will soon kiss.

STUMBLING UP YOUR STAIRCASE
is a good omen if you're wondering whether a
recent pairing will lead to lifelong love.

LIVING IN HARMONY

IF YOU TAKE BOTH MILK AND SUGAR
in your tea, put the sugar in before the milk in order
to avoid quarreling with your mate.

THE ANCIENT PERSIANS BELIEVED
a newly married couple should eat freshly caught,
fried fish on their wedding night.

IN ETHIOPIA, COUPLES EAT
as little as possible on their wedding day—
not only to avoid bathroom trips, but also
because it's believed to be lucky.

THE GIFTS OF ROMANCE

Many cultures believe that the gifts you give your partner are highly symbolic. Give your sweetheart tokens that will make him or her think only of you.

Some say you should avoid giving a lover shoes, since they could encourage the person to walk away.

Similarly, some believe that knitting socks or slippers for a lover will enable your beloved to run from you.

A bag might convince that person to pack up his or her things and go, and perfume or cologne could draw the attention of others.

To bind a lover to you forever, knit one of your own hairs into whatever you make for him or her.

CULTIVATING FIDELITY

"WASH AND WIPE TOGETHER,
stay in love forever." Enough said? Apparently not,
since others believe that a couple should avoid drying
themselves with the same bath towel after bathing, as sharing
could lead to a fight. Whether to perform intimate
hygiene habits together or separately seems
more a matter of personal preference
than superstition.

A WOMAN WHO IS WORRIED
that her mate will stray should prepare a delectable
feast of roast owl. Once the man eats the
meat, she need not worry again.

ANOTHER FEAST NOT FOR THE FAINT
of heart: Stir up a big bowl of steak tartare for
your love. In Ethiopia, eating raw meat is
said to boost one's sex drive.

IT MAY NOT BE THE MOST SUCCULENT
of foodstuffs, but lettuce is said to arouse
amorous feelings between two
people who eat it together.

DO NOT LET SOMEONE
remove a ring from your finger. Take it off yourself;
otherwise you could be tempting
your love to wander.

If a wife sews a swan's feather into her husband's pillow, he will notice only her.

FERTILITY

*Some couples who are having difficulty
getting pregnant go to the ends of the earth—literally—
by making a pilgrimage to Cerne Abbas, the well-endowed
giant that is carved into a hillside in Dorset, England,
or by trekking to Edinburgh's annual fertility
festival in April. But you need not venture
past your own front door.*

IN THE PHILIPPINES, A COUPLE TRYING
to have a baby is advised not to begin
construction on a new home until the seed
is planted. Doing so could make
conception more difficult.

WHEN YOU ARE TRYING

to get pregnant, it's best to situate your bed facing
east or west, rather than north or south.

* * *

A RABBIT'S FOOT IS A TOKEN

not only of luck but also of fertility, because
of the rabbit's famously prolific ability to reproduce.
Try nestling a rabbit's foot in your bedside table, then
stroking it gently each night before you retire.

* * *

IF YOU OR YOUR MATE SPIES

a group of jackdaws—dark, smooth-feathered
birds hailing from the crow family—from
your bedroom window, there's a good
chance a baby is on its way.

PREGNANCY

KEEP A KNIFE UNDER THE BED
of a pregnant woman in order to protect the
baby from ill will. As with the scissors-under-the-doormat
trick mentioned on page 76, those concerned about
safety can use an image of a knife rather than
an actual knife. The Chinese also believe
this will ease labor pains when
the big day comes.

STOCK A PREGNANT WOMAN'S PANTRY
with items she might crave—no matter how bizarre.
People from Trinidad and Tobago believe that a pregnant
woman should always indulge her cravings;
otherwise, her baby could be born with a
birthmark that looks just like the food
of which she deprived herself.

During antiquity, the tortoise was a symbol
of fertility. Surround an aspiring mother with
images of this reptile—decorate the bedroom
with a pair of handsome tortoise prints,
or seek out a sweet ceramic statue
to keep on her bedside table.

A mother-to-be longing to give birth to twins should eat twin bananas.

A PREGNANT WOMAN SHOULD NEVER SLEEP
in total darkness. Although the origin of this Chinese belief is
unclear, it seems to have something to do with creating fear
in the fetus's brand-new spirit. Another reason to invest
in a nightlight is that it would also significantly
decrease the risk of tripping during
midnight runs to the bathroom!

THE ANCIENT PERSIANS BELIEVED
a pregnant mother should carry around a small
linen sachet with wheat and a gold coin sewn into it.
The wheat signifies that the child will never go hungry,
and the gold coin that he or she will never suffer from
poverty. Instead of making a portable pouch,
consider sewing these two totems onto a
decorative pillow and placing it on
the mother-to-be's bed.

IN INDONESIA, IT IS BELIEVED
that pregnant women should look only at beautiful
pictures—and spend their time in beautiful surroundings—
so that their babies are born with good looks. Once you hear
news of a pregnancy, create an outdoor space filled with as
many plants as possible for the mother-to-be to enjoy. Clear
sitting rooms and bedrooms of clutter, and hang artwork the
pregnant woman loves in front of her favorite chairs.

THOUGH GINGER IS A TRADITIONAL REMEDY
for nausea in many cultures, Filipinos believe that
eating ginger just before you conceive can lead to
a child born with an extra finger or toe.

ONCE A PREGNANCY IS CONFIRMED,
be sure to rid the kitchen of any cups with cracks or
fissures. A pregnant woman should avoid drinking
from a cracked cup—to do so puts her in danger
of having a child with a cleft palate.

BABIES

IN TRINIDAD, THE UMBILICAL CORD
of a newborn baby is buried at the foot of a fruit tree
to ensure that the child will one day be able to bear
fruit as well. When your baby's cord falls off, you
can certainly save it and perform the same
ritual in your backyard. If this seems a
little too . . . corporeal, you can bury some other
totem, such as a lock of hair or a fingernail clipping.

NEVER LEAVE TWO BABIES
younger than forty days old alone in a room
with one another—even when they are sleeping.
Besides the obvious risks, the Turks believe that
one child will end up very short while
the other grows tall.

ASK AN INTELLIGENT PERSON TO GIVE
your baby his or her first haircut, then store a lock
of the cut hair in what you believe to be a brilliant book.
These two rituals aim to ensure that your child
is blessed with a gifted intellect.

SOME BELIEVE THAT BABIES BORN
feet first will have lifelong magical powers.

DON'T BUY A BABY GIFTS UNTIL
after it is born. Doing so would be akin to counting
your chickens before they hatch; meaning, in less
delicate terms, that you could risk the baby's health
in utero by preparing for it too early.

DON'T FRET IF YOUR BABY FALLS
out of bed—many think this means they will have a long life.

IF A DOG LICKS YOUR BABY,
don't worry; many believe this "baptism" will
make the baby a quick healer for life.

***

ACCORDING TO THE ANCIENT PERSIANS,
nursing mothers should consume lots of anise seed,
cinnamon, and sugar in order to keep their
milk abundant and sweet.

***

AFTER A BABY IS CIRCUMCISED,
hang a piece of turquoise jewelry over the head of his
crib or bassinet, and he will heal more quickly.

***

NEVER PASS AN OBJECT OVER A BABY'S HEAD;
this could stunt its growth. If this should happen inadvertently,
though, pull the baby's hair gently toward the sky.

TRAVELING RIGHT

*Even the happiest of clans has to get out
of the house sometimes.*

Some say that an itchy right foot foretells a voyage.

If you notice a spider sliding down its web in
the afternoon, you will soon take a trip.

Sleeping—at home—with your head to the
east means you will travel the world.

Russians believe that a person will travel
safely if those who remain at home refrain
from cleaning up the room of the departed until
they arrive at their destination.

When it rains as you're getting ready to leave a place, you're sure to return one day.

Indians consider the sight of an elephant when you're on a trip to be very auspicious—the elephant is thought to be a representative of Ganesh, the god of good luck.

If you see dung, cotton, or hay at the beginning of a journey—according to Indian tradition—you have every reason to believe it will go well.

Taking a cat on a sea voyage will bring luck. For the people on the ship, anyway. It's hard to know what such an experience might do to a cat.

CHILDREN

WE SOMETIMES NEED TO LEAVE CHILDREN ALONE
for a split second, whether to go to the bathroom or tend
to another child in need. Obviously, this should be avoided at all
costs, but should you need to bolt momentarily, place a
broom next to the child you leave. The Turkish
believe the broom will offer protection.

WHEN A FRIEND'S CHILD VISITS YOUR HOME
for the first time, give him or her a bag of rice as a
symbolic wish that they never go hungry.

HANG A CORNO—

an Italian horn-shaped charm—from
your child's "vehicle"—bicycle, tricycle, or wagon—
to protect it from accidents. These are available at
most jewelry stores, in both pricey
and inexpensive varieties.

PROMOTING HEALTH IN YOUR HOME

IN MANY OBVIOUS WAYS, A PERSON'S health begins at home. Home is the place where we receive rest, nourishment, and kinship—three things that promote good health more than anything else. In this section, you'll find practices and rituals that aim to keep you and your loved ones at home, rather than in the hospital (which, given its propensity to make sick people even sicker, could likely benefit from a consultation with a feng shui master).

ORIENT A SICK PERSON'S BED NORTH-SOUTH,
not east-west, according to Irish folklore, and they
will get well more quickly.

RATTLESNAKE SKINS WARD OFF DISEASE.
Nestle one under the sheet of a sick person's bed,
or place it on his or her bedside table.

TO PROTECT THEMSELVES
from catching contagious illnesses, the Greeks
make a *filahta*—a small cloth pouch filled with medallions,
dirt, stones, and lucky herbs—and pin it to their clothing.

COLDS

ON THE FIRST DAY OF FALL,
catch a leaf in midair, and you won't catch a cold all season.

TIE A RED ONION TO THE BEDPOST
to keep colds away from children. Appalachian mothers do.

AMBER BEADS CAN BE
a formidable opponent to colds—both to fight them
off and to cure them once they are caught.

MANY ITALIANS BELIEVE
that exposing oneself to a cold draft can lead to
health problems worse than the common cold. Some won't
open a window, even in a stuffy summer room.

COLIC

—————

CARRY A BABY AROUND THE HOUSE THREE TIMES
before putting it to bed to prevent it from crying all night.

COUGH

—————

Try the following to get rid of a cough:

Get very close to a horse's mouth and inhale its breath.

Drink a cup of donkey's milk.

Stew an owl and drink the broth.

*(Since donkeys and owls are fairly hard to come by,
you may substitute chicken broth for the second and third
remedies. At the very least, chicken broth has been scientifi-
cally proven to contain strong disease-fighting compounds.)*

CROUP

MAKE THE BABY A NECKLACE

of coral beads (just be sure to remove it when no
adult will be in attendance). This will calm the baby's
coughing and allow it to get some rest.

FEVER

PLACE HALF AN ONION,

cut-side up, under the bed of the overheated
person. This will cause the fever to break. When
the person's sense of smell returns enough for them
to wrinkle his or her nose at the onion, the person
is well enough for it to be removed.

HEADACHES

CUTTING YOUR HAIR ON GOOD FRIDAY
is said to prevent headaches for the rest of the year.

HICCUPS

IF THE HICCUP-AFFLICTED ONE IS A CHILD,
remove a string from his or her mother's clothing
and apply it to the child's forehead.

Adults seeking a cure for their hiccups should stare intensely at a horseshoe, or put a spoonful of sugar on their tongue until it dissolves.

Acorns are a symbol of a long life, so incorporate them into your decor—either artfully arranged in a pretty bowl, or incorporated into a print on bed linens or a tablecloth.

LONGEVITY

SLEEPING WITH YOUR HEAD
to the south can lead to a long life.

IN THE MIDDLE AGES,
many families kept a white horse to ward off death.
If you don't have your own stables, there's no reason
why your white horse can't be stuffed.

NOSEBLEEDS

TO STOP A NOSEBLEED,
thread string through a piece of bread and place it
around the person's neck like a pendant.

TO KEEP THE NOSEBLEED FROM RETURNING,
tie a red string around the patient's
neck or little finger.

PLAGUE

MANY PEOPLE BELIEVE THE BUBONIC PLAGUE
is extinct, but it's recently been identified in places such
as Los Angeles and New York. To repel it, place a
dead spider inside a walnut shell, and wear
it as an amulet around your neck.

RHEUMATISM

TO PREVENT RHEUMATISM,
sleep with your shoes tucked under the edge of the bed,
or carry a nutmeg seed or a potato in your pocket.

TO CURE RHEUMATISM,
place an iron or brass ring on the fourth finger of the afflicted.

WHAT DOES THIS SNEEZE MEAN TO YOU?

Everybody sneezes. whether it's from allergies, black pepper, emerging from a dim theater on a sunny day, or one of these listed reasons.

Ancient greek tradition dictates that a sneeze draws attention to the truth. So when you sneeze, think back to your last thought or utterance— it's just been validated.

A Japanese and Vietnamese belief is that when someone sneezes, he or she is being spoken of.

In India, if one sneezes uncontrollably just before embarking on an important task, the persons takes a drink of water to begin the task anew.

SNEEZING

TO PREVENT A SNEEZE, SAY A WORD
with many syllables just as you feel the sneeze about to
come. But only use this in the most dire of circumstances.
Most sneezes are for a reason.

SORE THROAT

TIE A DIRTY KNEESOCK
around your neck to alleviate the pain of a sore throat.
Many say a silk cord will do the same thing, and it
looks—and smells—a lot better.

IN THE MIDDLE AGES, A COMMON REMEDY
to ease the swelling and pain of a sore throat was to tie the right paw of a wolf around the neck. Since wolf paws are difficult to come by these days, consider choosing a kneesock (dirty or not) with a wolf-paw print, or stringing a wolf-paw charm on a silk cord instead.

SPLINTERS

USE CLAY AS A POULTICE
to draw splinters out. Some also say this works to extract poisons, such as those from insect bites.

STOMACHACHE

AN IRISH HOME REMEDY
for stomachache is to tie a sachet of mint around the wrist.

STY

TO HEAL A STY, TOUCH THE AFFECTED EYE
three times with a piece of gold—preferably,
your mother's wedding ring.

PULL OUT AN EYELASH
from the affected eye.

RUB THE STY
with the tail of a black cat.

YOU'VE HEARD ABOUT BLUES-MUSIC SHOWDOWNS
that take place at a crossroads. Well, sometimes the
cure for a pesky sty can be found there, too.
Next time you have a sty, venture beyond your
four walls, and get yourself to the nearest crossroads
(most likely just at the end of your block). Then recite
this old rhyme, which many believe will have you seeing
clearly in seconds: "Sty, sty, leave my eye.
Take the next one coming by!"

THRUSH

HOLD A FROG'S HEAD
in the open mouth of the afflicted. If this isn't
possible, locate a nearby French bistro that serves
frogs legs and request an order to go.

WARTS

TIE THE SAME NUMBER OF KNOTS

in a string as you have warts. Toss it over your left shoulder
and don't look back at it. Your warts will soon disappear.

BURY A ROOSTER'S COMB

or a piece of bacon in your backyard to get rid of warts.

DRAW A PICTURE OF A WART,

then burn the paper in your fireplace.

PEEL AN APPLE, RUB IT ON THE WART,

and feed it to a pig. Your wart will disappear.

Bringing Friendship and Joy into Your Home

ALTHOUGH WE'VE ALL AGREED AT
times with F. Scott Fitzgerald's pithy insight
that "Nothing is as obnoxious as other people's
luck," most would admit that a healthy circle
of friends is the most important ingredient
for surviving life's trials—both big and
little. These ideas will help you retain the
relationships that hold you together, whether
you're celebrating a special occasion, or
just sharing an intimate cup of tea.

SHOULD A FRIEND GIVE

you a gift of knives, politely decline—they are
said to put a sharp hex on even the soundest friendship.
If declining is simply impossible, offer the giver
a coin in exchange for the gift.

THE GERMANS BELIEVE

that if your right ear itches, a friend is speaking
well of you. (If your left ear itches, they may
be speaking ill of you.)

THE SCOTTISH BELIEVE

that the appearance of an unfamiliar dog at the front
door signals the beginnings of a wonderful new
friendship (with a person, not the dog!).

Never leave a pair of scissors open—
this can create discord between roommates
or members of a household.

SHOULD YOU STUMBLE

on your way up the stairs, you may expect to receive a letter from a long-lost friend. The same is true if you find a bay leaf in your soup bowl.

IF YOU FEEL SOMEONE WISHES YOU ILL,

remove your jacket and then put it back on in the opposite way you usually put it on.

TRY NOT TO SHAKE HANDS

over a threshold. A doorway is not the most auspicious place to give a gift, either.

WHEN VISITORS COME TO CALL,

never greet them in your bedroom. Always pull yourself together and receive them in a public part of your home. Failing to do so could augur that you'll become bedridden in the future.

IF YOU INADVERTENTLY LET TEA BREW
too long and it's too strong for your taste,
you will soon meet a new friend.

THE BRITISH BELIEVE
that a friend who cannot seem to cut a slice of bread evenly
is lying to whomever they are about to serve.

IF A SPIDER CREEPS TOWARD YOU,
or a needle sticks upright in the floor, you may expect a letter.

WEARING TOPAZ IS A WAY TO ATTRACT
many friends; so is incorporating touches of topaz
into your decor. Look for napkin rings ornamented with the
stone, or keep a small bowl of decorative topaz
crystals in your living room.

Each stray button you find when cleaning out your closet or drawers means a new friendship.

SHOULD YOU ENCOUNTER
an abandoned silk fan in front of your house, spruce
up your formal wardrobe. In Japan, such a discovery
means a person can expect to become close to—
or a part of—a noble family.

SALT IS A SYMBOL OF FRIENDSHIP,
so try not to spill it. If you do, immediately toss
some over your left shoulder.

IN AFGHANISTAN, IT'S BELIEVED
that if your broom touches your own feet while
you're sweeping, a friend might soon falsely
accuse you of something.

SOMEONE WHO MENDS A TORN GARMENT
while still wearing it will likely be spoken about
behind his or her back by a good friend.

ANIMAL COMPANIONS

Dogs aren't the only animals that function as a person's best friend. Here are ways to keep these crucial members of your social circle happy— and how to decode messages they might be trying to send you.

DOGS ARE SAID TO HAVE

a highly developed sixth sense. They are unwilling to walk into an area that's haunted. So for those with a great fear of the supernatural, a pet pooch can provide a welcome insurance policy.

SOME BELIEVE THAT CATS SHOULD

be kept away from newborns, as they could rob the child of their breath.

CATS CAN HAVE A HARD TIME
adjusting when their owners move to a new house.
Some believe that if they are brought into the
new house through a window rather than
a door, they will not run away.

WHEN A CAT SITS BEFORE A GROUP
of people and cleans her face, the first person
she looks at will marry soon.

THINK TWICE BEFORE KEEPING A TURTLE
as a pet. In Thailand, someone who sets a
turtle free will be cured of their depression. If you
can't stand the idea of saying good-bye to your pet turtle,
don't fret—the Chinese believe that simply rubbing
his shell will bring good fortune.

IF YOU KEEP EGG-LAYING CHICKENS,
never burn the shells in the fireplace, or your
hens will give you no more eggs.

IN ANCIENT EGYPT,
animals were so highly regarded that some
were regularly adorned with jewelry. Cats wore gold,
and dogs wore silver. If you want to reward your
pet, treat it to a silver or gold collar. It may
conjure fond cellular memories of its
forebears' lives in antiquity.

FEEDING YOUR FRIENDS AND FAMILY

"Some folk want their luck buttered." —Thomas Hardy

The preparation of food has long carried symbolic meaning. You've heard that the way to a man's heart is through his stomach—well, the stomach is a good way to get to the heart of every other loved one, too. In this section, you'll find out how to make your kitchen work best for you, and also how to best enjoy the fruits (and vegetables) of your labor.

IN OLD GERMANY, MANY INSISTED that an older woman cook the first meal on a young bride's new stove. This stemmed from the belief that there were angry elves hiding inside the oven, and only the older woman could successfully scare them off.

If you find a hot pepper in a dish you're cooking—and you don't remember adding it— pay special attention, as danger could lurk nearby.

INADVERTENTLY BURNING ONIONS
is not all bad—make a wish during this culinary fiasco
and it will come true.

NEVER STIR WITH A FORK—
some believe this stirs up trouble. Use a
spoon or whisk instead.

ALWAYS STIR CLOCKWISE;
otherwise your dish—and your evening—
could turn out badly.

A YIDDISH SUPERSTITION HOLDS
that one's oven should never be empty; even when
it's not being used, keep a pan inside so it will be full forever
(figuratively speaking, of course).

IN SOME LATINO FAMILIES,
angry or upset people are discouraged from
opening the refrigerator door for fear the heat
they emit might spoil the food.

INADVERTENTLY PUTTING ON
an apron inside-out means that something
wonderful is on the way.

CUT A CROSS INTO THE SURFACE
of bread before you bake it so the devil
can escape as the bread rises.

SHOULD BAKED APPLES EXPLODE
in the oven, you may be facing a night without
dessert, but you can also look forward
to good fortune on the way.

SHARING A MEAL

ITALIANS SAY YOU SHOULD NEVER PLACE
a loaf of bread upside down. Since the devil "escapes"
from the bread when it's right-side up, turning it
over could trap his evil energy.

IT IS WISE TO EAT A WHOLE FISH
from head to tail, not the other way around. By
respecting the natural direction of things—head to tail
symbolizing "beginning to end"—you can rest assured
your family will enjoy many more fish in the future.

IN INDONESIA, EATING RICE
from a small plate is said to cause tension between
family members. So be sure to give those chopsticks
plenty of room to move around.

COMPANY'S COMING!

*There are scores of signs that visitors are on the way.
Make an extra pound of pasta if . . .*

A large flaming chunk of wood flies out of a fire

A broom falls across a door

Someone drops a needle and can't pick it up

Someone drops a dishcloth (the number of people
coming may be found in the number of
folds in the dishcloth)

Someone sneezes before breakfast—or simply
complains of an itchy nose

You notice yourself taking another helping of food
that's already present on your plate

There are many beliefs about the meaning of inadvertently dropping a piece of cutlery. An old rhyme notes a few: "Knife falls, gentleman calls. Fork falls, lady calls. Spoon falls, baby calls."

If you have human visitors or houseguests you'd like to see leave—perhaps a nosy neighbor whose "welcome" is unwelcome—sprinkle a bit of salt behind them when they're not looking, and they'll soon be on their way, unlikely to return. Placing a broom upside down behind the front door will also encourage unwelcome visitors to make themselves scarce.

CHILDREN IN INDONESIA ARE ENCOURAGED
to eat lots of chicken wings if they want to travel to
distant lands. While it is difficult to find the origin
of this belief, one might presume it has something to
do with the fact that wings are for flying.

IN ENGLAND, MANY BELIEVE
that you should push out the bottom of a boiled
egg's shell before eating it, creating a "tunnel" through
which water—or demonic energy—can pass.
They call this "letting the devil out."

SHOULD A FISH BONE GET STUCK
in your mouth, enlist the help of a breech-born person.
Who knows why, but he or she will have no trouble
removing it. If there is no breech-born person
nearby, try pulling on your big toe.

NEVER CUT BOTH ENDS OFF
a loaf of bread. Start with one, and move toward
the other. In addition to delaying the bread's
process of going stale, this is thought
to keep away bad luck.

IN GREECE, LEFTOVER BREAD
is never thrown away. Doing so would be
wasteful and would tempt fate to deprive your
family of surplus bread in the future. Make croutons
or breadcrumbs with it, or feed the ducks.

WHEN A FLY LANDS IN YOUR FOOD,
it's good luck. (Don't worry—you don't have to eat it!)

DRINKING

—◦◦◦◦◦—

IF YOU DROP A GLASS
and it doesn't break, you're in for a day of good luck.

—◦◦◦—

IF BUBBLES APPEAR IN THE CENTER
of the surface of your coffee or tea, money
may come to you soon.

—◦◦◦—

WHEN THE LABEL STAPLED TO THE STRING
that holds your tea bag comes loose, you're destined
to lose something important within a week.

—◦◦◦—

GERMANS BELIEVE
that if you sing while brewing beer,
the results will be delicious.

PARTIES

*You most likely know that it's best to avoid
having a guest list totaling thirteen. But do you
know why? Reasons for this superstition span cultural
traditions. Judas was the thirteenth guest at the
Last Supper—and we all know what happened there.
A Norse myth also involves a meal in which the thirteenth
guest was Loki, the god of mischief. That dinner party
ended in the death of Balder, the god of happiness.
The moral? Shoot for guest lists of twelve or
fourteen people. It's good to have a neighbor
who's always willing to be your "Lucky 14" and
dine at a moment's notice. In fact, the French have
a name for this person—le quatorzien.*

RUSSIANS BELIEVE A BIRTHDAY PARTY
should never be thrown before the birthday itself,
lest the happy day fail to arrive.

NEVER SEAT UNMARRIED PEOPLE AT THE CORNERS
of the table, or they could stay unmarried forever.

IF YOU ARE FORCED TO CONTEND
with a wine-drunk guest, feed the person lettuce to sober
him or her up. With its minimal caloric content, lettuce
won't have much of an impact on blood sugar,
so if this one works, you know it's magic!

SHOULD SOMEONE ASK YOU TO PASS
him a knife, place it down on the table in front of him
instead of handing it to him directly, which
could spawn a quarrel.

Spilling wine at the dinner table is widely considered to be bad luck. To reverse things, just dab a little behind each of your ears.

NEVER TASTE SOMETHING
directly from a knife—this will create anger.

***

WHOEVER TAKES THE LAST PIECE
of bread from the table will find a mate
who is very good-looking.

***

IN RUSSIA, WHEN ALCOHOL IS BEING POURED,
some should be given to all guests, even if they
do not plan to drink. Russians also advise
against filling a glass held in the air—
place it on the table before pouring.

***

DO NOT POUR WINE BACKHANDED—
in Russia, such a gesture insults the
person receiving the wine.

THE ROMANS BELIEVED

that fire should not be a topic of conversation
at dinner. If, however, it does come up, spilling
some water on the table will eliminate
any danger it poses.

ACCORDING TO OLD PERSIAN CUSTOM,

when an important guest finishes dinner, he should be
presented with a few more bites of meat. If he is too
full to eat them, another dinner party has to be thrown
the next night. So if you're not a professional event
planner, maybe it's best to leave your
guests just the littlest bit hungry.

HOLIDAYS

———◦◦◦———

The word "holiday" comes from the Old English word
haligdæg, *meaning "holy day." Some of the following*
traditions are God-fearing, and some are not. All,
however, will contribute to your family's revelry
on those rare days when everyone can
be home at the same time.

– NEW YEAR'S –

JUST AFTER THE STROKE OF MIDNIGHT,
invite a tall, handsome visitor into your home. His most
important characteristic? Dark brown hair. (It is said that
blonds and redheads can usher in bad luck.)

ALSO AT THE STROKE OF MIDNIGHT,
open all the doors and windows of the house to let the
old year out and the new one in.

MAKE LOTS OF NOISE,

not just in celebration, but also to scare away any evil.

DROP SOMETHING MADE OF GOLD

into your glass of champagne, then drink from the glass.
Just don't swallow the bauble!

EAT TWELVE GRAPES AT MIDNIGHT.

Each one corresponds to a month of the new year, and its
sweetness will predict the sweetness of its month.
In Peru, a thirteenth grape is always eaten—for luck.

IN CHILE, LENTILS ARE CUSTOMARY

as a midnight snack on the first day of the year.
On New Year's Eve, Chileans also write down all the things
that were bad about the previous year, then burn
the list up so history doesn't repeat itself.

PERUVIANS EMPLOY A POTATO
fortune-telling technique to predict what
the new year holds for their finances. They
take three potatoes, leaving one with its skin on,
peeling one halfway, and peeling the third completely.
They then hide the potatoes under the sofa at the
beginning of New Year's Eve. When the clock strikes
midnight, they reach under the couch and grab a
potato without looking. The more skin on
the potato, the more financial
success in the year ahead.

IN THE PHILIPPINES,
polka dots represent money. Therefore, wearing
polka-dotted garments on New Year's is a way to
foment your earning power.

You're destined for 365 days of bliss
when the first butterfly you see in
the new year is white.

A MORE OFFBEAT PERUVIAN TRADITION:
standing naked before a shaman and being
sprayed with a mouthful of chamomile tea.
This means good luck in the new year, and
it also inspires a significant amount
of hilarity to kick it off.

IN ITALY, WEARING RED UNDERWEAR
on New Year's means you'll have a nice time behind
closed doors for the rest of the year.

SOME ITALIAN AMERICANS
eat sauerkraut on New Year's Day and hide a
dime in it. Whoever finds the dime will
have good luck all year.

IN MANY ASIAN COUNTRIES,
it is traditional to slurp endless yards of noodles
on New Year's Day in order to have a long life.
These noodles should be as long as possible,
so prepare for some deep breaths.

YOU PROBABLY KNOW THAT
it's an African American tradition to serve black-eyed
peas on New Year's Day. But did you know
that it is a Brazilian tradition as well?
In Brazil, lentils signify wealth.

FATTY PORK DISHES ARE TRADITIONALLY
enjoyed on New Year's Day across a number
of Eastern cultures because they
symbolize living off the fat of the land.

MANY PEOPLE BELIEVE

that the first day of the new year sets the tone
for the other 364 days. Accordingly:

Tolerate more from your children than you
would normally. You don't want them to begin the
year feeling resentful after a scolding.

Never remove anything from the home
on New Year's Day. Wait until January 2 to take
the garbage out—this symbolizes that the family
will not lose possessions over the course of
the new year, only gain them.

Wear only new clothes—and you'll get many
more as the year progresses.

Be very careful not to break anything.

– BIRTHDAYS –

MANY PEOPLE HOLD A SIMILAR BELIEF
about birthdays that they do about New Year's Day—
that this day sets the tone for the rest of the year.
In the Philippines, rice noodles are served on
birthdays to symbolize long life.

– VALENTINE'S DAY –

THE ELIZABETHANS BELIEVED
that, in order to find love, a single girl should
pin five bay leaves to her pillow on
the eve of Valentine's Day.

– GOOD FRIDAY –

THE BRITISH BELIEVE
that bread baked on this holy day will never
grow mold. So pull out the rolling pin
and get kneading!

– EASTER –

FOR CHRISTIANS, THE EASTER HOLIDAY
represents rebirth. Wearing new clothes
to celebrate will bring newness all year around.

SOME IN THE AMERICAN MIDWEST BELIEVE
that if those with freckles wash their faces
with the morning dew before sunrise on
Easter, the freckles will disappear.

– MAY DAY –

DENIZENS OF THE DEEP SOUTH MAINTAIN
that holding a mirror over a well on the First of May will
reveal the image of your future husband or wife.

– HALLOWEEN –

TO KEEP EVIL SPIRITS AWAY
on the scariest day of the year, walk
around your house backward three times
in a counterclockwise direction.

A YOUNG WOMAN SHOULD LOOK
into a mirror in her home at midnight on
Halloween if she desires to see the
face of her future husband.

Feng shui masters often say that hanging
a dried wreath on your door blocks
chi from the entrance.

– CHRISTMAS –

ON THIS DAY, THE GERMANS TIE
together two fruit trees to "marry" them, thus
encouraging them to bear more fruit.

IN GREECE, IT IS BELIEVED
that scores of little goblins called *Kalikatzaroi*
invade the home during the twelve days of Christmas.
While they do not cause any real harm, they do cause mischief—
scratches on the walls are a sure sign that they're about.
To repel them, dip a cross into holy water spiked with
basil and sprinkle it on all the entrances to the house.
Not all the actions of the Kalikatzaroi are bad,
though—sometimes they leave treats,
such as nuts, for the children.

GENERATING
WEALTH
IN
YOUR HOME

WHILE MONEY TO BURN CAN SEEM LIKE the best gift in the world, many of our greatest philosophers warned against the dangers of unbridled prosperity. Heraclitus said that "no one that encounters prosperity does not also encounter danger." Victor Hugo surmised that "adversity makes men, and prosperity makes monsters." Still, few of us would turn away from an outstretched hand offering cash. The ideas that follow aim to help attract fortune to you and your family. Just remember, in the immortal words of Confucius, "When prosperity comes, do not use all of it."

GOOD SIGNS

———◦◦◦◦———

IF YOU DISCOVER AN ANT'S NEST

near your front door, you can look forward to
coming into some money.

———

FINDING A SPIDER

on your clothes means a windfall is at hand.

———

WHEN TEA LEAVES FLOAT

to the top of the pot, wealth will soon show up, too.

IF YOU NOTICE YOUR LEFT HAND ITCHING,
money will soon be on its way.

IF YOU NOTICE A SPIDER
spinning its web, you'll soon find your closet
overflowing with new clothes. Whether they'll come
as gifts, or you'll simply be overwhelmed by a need to
go shopping, you'll have to wait to find out.

MAKING MONEY

***

TO INCREASE A FATHER'S FORTUNE,
Turkish custom suggests taking a lock of hair from his son's
first haircut and putting it in the father's pocket.

TO MAKE SOME EXTRA CASH,
eat your bread buttered-side down.

THE ANCIENT GREEKS BELIEVED
that if you ask a bird where to find a treasure, it will
fly directly to a spot where precious metals can be found.
Don't worry if you feel uncomfortable talking to a bird;
just make sure no one but the bird is listening. Even
if someone does hear you, the reward is likely
to be worth the humiliation.

IF, WHEN ENJOYING THE FRESH AIR
in your backyard on a crisp evening, you see a falling
star, say the word "money" three times
and wait for the coins to roll in.

IF YOU'RE IN THE MARKET
for a used car, consider purchasing one from
a prosperous owner. The car could attract
money to you as well.

HANG A FULL-LENGTH MIRROR
on the outside of your bathroom door to attract
wealth. It may seem strange to hang it on the outside
rather than the inside, but since the bathroom is
the one place in the house where everything
"goes down the toilet," the goal of the
mirror is to reflect and draw in
energy circulating outside the bathroom.

BABY WARBUCKS

PARENTS SHOULD BURY THE PLACENTA
of the newborn in the backyard, near the
back of the house. Indonesians believe this will
ensure the baby never lacks money.

HOME BUSINESS

IT MAY TURN YOUR STOMACH,
but finding a mouse's nest in your home office means
success in business is on the way.

IF YOU DO BUSINESS AT HOME,
do not keep a pet turtle. It is a Chinese belief
that, because turtles move slowly, your business
will grow slowly with a turtle around.

When you welcome a new addition into your family, press a silver coin into his or her palm. This gesture ensures the child will never suffer from poverty.

KEEPING MONEY

NEVER PLACE YOUR PURSE
on the floor. Doing so could result in the
loss of all your money.

YOU'VE UNDOUBTEDLY HEARD
it's rude to whistle indoors, but did you also
know it can be hazardous to your bank account?
Russian tradition espouses that when you whistle
indoors you whistle away your wealth.

NEVER SWEEP UNDER SOMEONE'S FEET—
you'll sweep away his earning potential.

TAKING THE TRASH OUT

at night could lead to a loss of material wealth.

IF YOUR BAG IS EMPTY OF MONEY,

don't let moonlight shine in it, or it may

never see another dime.

Attracting Luck to Your Home

AS HUMAN BEINGS, MANY OF US CLING
to the hope (or fear) that much of what
happens in our lives is beyond our control.
As the great Roman poet and philosopher Ovid
said, "Luck affects everything. Let your hook
always be cast; in the stream where you
least expect it there will be a fish."
This feeling of wild anticipation is what
propels many of us through life's darkest hours.

Still, the concept of luck has many enemies.
Thomas Jefferson said, "I find that the harder I
work, the more luck I seem to have." He is right
in believing it is not wise to depend entirely on
fortune. But as poet Judith Viorst once said,
"Superstition is foolish, childish, primitive,
and irrational—but how much
does it cost you to knock on wood?"

Here, then, are a few ways to gently coax
good luck in your direction.

FUN AND GAMES

IF YOU WANT TO WIN
at cards, the Irish suggest you stick a crooked
pin inside your coat. Or, walk around your
chair before your hand is dealt.

MANY RUSSIANS BELIEVE
that a single woman lucky at cards will be
unlucky in love, but that a married woman
who is lucky at cards will bring her
husband luck as well.

DAYS OF THE WEEK

Every day can be a good day if you know what to do when.

– SUNDAY –

A very auspicious day for a child to be born

Not a good day to wash a bread knife

– MONDAY –

Sets the tone for the rest of the week, so beware
of hard work and company—unless you don't mind working
and entertaining for seven days straight

– TUESDAY –

A project begun on this day may have a
difficult time coming to fruition

– WEDNESDAY –

Perhaps the best day for medical appointments
and procedures, or to write a letter asking for help

– THURSDAY –

Cutting your fingernails on this day can
bring good things over the weekend

– FRIDAY –

Not the best day to begin a quilt—or any
other creative or crafty project

– SATURDAY –

Cutting nails could lead to disappointment
(so much for weekend mani-pedis!)

In Renaissance Florence, Saturday was believed
to be the day when significant events occurred—both good and
bad. So to be safe, avoid planning anything major on
Saturday for fear it could go off track

NUMBERS

As any mathematician will tell you, numbers are everywhere, but nowhere are they more noticeable than in our homes. Pay attention to the elements of your house that evoke numerics: from how many steps make up your staircase to the integers comprising your address itself. Also pay attention to the dates on which you plan important home events, and the number of items with which you decorate.

DID YOU KNOW THAT ITALIANS BELIEVE

that Friday the 17th—not Friday the 13th—is the unluckiest day? So refrain from hosting any get-togethers when Friday and the 17th of the month coincide.

IN RUSSIA, A BOUQUET MUST ALWAYS CONTAIN
an odd number of flowers—unless it
is destined for a funeral.

FOR SOME REASON, IN MANY CULTURES,
odd numbers rather than even ones are believed to be
lucky. This is not true in the Chinese culture, though—they
favor even numbers, and they consider the most auspicious
number to be 8. In fact, the Chinese believe that the safest
license plates and most desirable addresses are
those containing this number.

ON THE OTHER HAND, MANY ASIAN CULTURES
consider the least auspicious number to be 4.
The number 14 is not particularly positive,
either—it evokes death.

GOOD OMENS

Encountering a pile of hay

Stubbing your right toe

Finding a piece of coral somewhere far
away from the sea

Tripping over a broom handle

Losing a stocking
(you'll find a present)

Wearing your shoes out at the heel
(you will be rich)

Wearing your shoes out at the sides
(you will be wise)

WISH MAKING

*You probably know about stars and wells,
but there are so many other good times to make
a wish! Here are a few of them:*

Before the first robin of spring flies away

Seeing a red-haired girl riding a white horse

Coming unexpectedly upon a chimney sweep

Climbing a tree in which a cuckoo bird is crying

Before crossing a snake's path

When eating the first pick of any fruit of the season

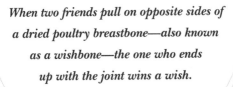

When two friends pull on opposite sides of
a dried poultry breastbone—also known
as a wishbone—the one who ends
up with the joint wins a wish.

Here are some more proactive wish-making scenarios:

In the Japanese shinto tradition, believers create
shrines hung with *ema*, little wooden plaques on which
they inscribe a wish. Why not create a secular version of
this shrine at home, and encourage everyone
in the family to contribute?

If you can stand to hold a lit match in your fingertips until
it burns out entirely, you have earned a wish.

Blow a wish at a pile of hay

Count one hundred white horses

If you find a nail—and you're fortunate enough not to
step on it—make a wish and hammer it into something
in order for your wish to come true. But don't pick the
nail up if it's rusty—it still foretells good luck,
just leave it where you found it.

ANIMALS

Since the beginning of human civilization, animals
have represented a powerful connection to the
spirit world. Few celebrate at the sight of a bug indoors.
But finding any of the following visitors
in your home brings good fortune:

A grasshopper

A bee

A group of three butterflies

A cricket

These signs from the animal kingdom bode well, too:

The sound of a cat sneezing

Encountering a herd of cattle on the road

A bird call coming from the west

Encountering a spotted dog on the way to a meeting

A ladybug that lands on your hand; the deeper its color,
the more luck it will bring

A bird relieving itself on your head

The sight of a flock of wild geese taking off into the air

Storks building a nest in one's chimney

A colt running toward you

Finding a lizard's discarded tail

A blackbird making its nest atop your home

Getting hit in the head by a bat
(the animal, not the sporting implement)

The hum of bees
(ancient Greeks believed it was a hymn of praise)

DON'T WORRY IF A BLACK CAT CROSSES
your path. Just tie a knot in a string, and any
bad luck will vanish with the cat.

*If you are a knitter, avoid storing your
needles stabbed through a skein of yarn.
Some believe that anyone wearing an item
made from the stabbed yarn will
be plagued by misfortune.*

MAKING YOUR OWN LUCK: WHAT NOT TO DO

All these inadvertent gestures can lead to bad luck, so be aware when carrying out your everyday activities.

NEVER LEAN A BROOM

against a bed, and never place a hat on top of a bed. Both are thought to augur death.

KEEP YOUR SHOES OFF THE TABLE

for the same reason as above—shoes atop a table conjure up images of a dead body on a mortuary slab.

DON'T WALK THROUGH A DOOR
leading with your left foot. You know what they say
about putting your "right" foot forward.

PASSING BY A MAGPIE
is thought to be bad luck in England.
Should you come across one, tip your hat—
either a real or imaginary one—
to avert any negativity.

WE'VE ALL HEARD
that breaking a mirror can lead to seven years
of bad luck. But a reversal of fortune is within reach:
just gather all the shards and bury them.
The misfortune will be buried, too.

*They say that bought bees never prosper, so if
you're planning to become a beekeeper, be sure
to secure your hive via gifts or barter,
not the exchange of currency.*

MANY CULTURES BELIEVE

that leaving a white tablecloth on your dining
table overnight is a bad idea—probably because
it looks reminiscent of a funeral shroud. To be safe,
toss it in the wash before you hit the hay—
or stick to more festive table linens.

NEVER TEMPT THE EVIL EYE

by boasting. If you do, touch wood three times.

OPALS, IN GENERAL, ARE UNLUCKY STONES

to possess, except by those born in October.

THE ANCIENT PERSIANS BELIEVED

it was a terrible idea to remove either fire or water from
the house at sunset. Transporting these most sacred of forces
as the sun was going down was thought to bring bad luck.